KIP SYDNEY

IMPROVE MONEY MANAGEMENT

The Ultimate Guide to Money Management for
Millennials, Learn How You Can Save and Invest Your
Money and Prevent Falling Into Debt

Descrierea CIP a Bibliotecii Naţionale a României
KIP SYDNEY
    IMPROVE MONEY MANAGEMENT. The Ultimate Guide to Money Management for Millennials, Learn How You Can Save and Invest Your Money and Prevent Falling Into Debt / Kip Sydney – Bucharest: Editura My Ebook, 2021
    ISBN

KIP SYDNEY

IMPROVE MONEY MANAGEMENT

The Ultimate Guide to Money Management for
Millennials, Learn How You Can Save and Invest Your
Money and Prevent Falling Into Debt

My Ebook Publishing House
Bucharest, 2021

When it comes to learning about money management, millennials are forging their own way for good reasons – the main one being that things are totally different now than they used to be. The fact is, millennials face completely different financial issues than the generations before them.

Millennials are defined as the individuals born between 1981 and 1997, and are also known as Generation Y. This generation is the largest generation. They are very diverse, as only about 40 percent of them identify as non-Hispanic whites. They are more likely to get married later in life, and they like to live in metropolitan areas rather than in rural areas. Additionally, they're not as drawn to materialistic trappings as their older counterparts. However, that may be due to the money challenges that they face.

Money Challenges Millennials Face

Gen Y faces hard realities when it comes to student debt, low wages, high rents, and the high cost of health insurance and health care today. Thankfully, even with these challenges, millennials overall like managing their personal finances and are confident about their ability to do so, even with the frustrations mentioned.

Statistically, millennials are saving more for retirement than past generations. They have learned from watching their parents burn through their own retirement savings during the Great Recession. In fact, according to the TransAmerica Center for Retirement Studies, 70 percent of millennials started saving for retirement around the age of 22.

They are also saving money for other reasons and tend to dislike using credit as much as their parents. The main problem isn't willingness – it's low wages. Due to this fact, they need to save more than the average of 8 to 10 percent of their salaries each year to ensure their retirements are safe. Because unlike past generations, millennials aren't relying on the government to provide that retirement, since they are overall very distrustful of the government.

Even with all the positive information that the research shows regarding millennials and money in terms of their knowledge and desire to use money wisely, the importance of both retirement savings and emergency fund savings for this generation must be stressed. Having an emergency savings will ensure that Gen Y can avoid raiding their retirement accounts like many of their parents had to, due to high consumer debt and low short-term emergency savings available for them.

Every smart money decision you make starts with creating a realistic budget, so let's look at that next.

Create a Budget the Easy Way

Many people think creating a budget is a long and challenging process. But the truth is, a budget is just a plan and guideline that you follow to ensure that you end up where you want to be financially. Without a budget, you may make choices based on erroneous assumptions. With a budget, you can make financial decisions based on reality.

Add Up Your Income

Your budget starts with your income. You need to know how much money you actually have to spend each month. You can add up your gross income, or your net income if you remember only to budget the money you really have access to.

For example, if you have your own business and your income is $50,000 a year after business expenses, you still have to pay taxes (including self-employment tax) from that, which means you don't have $50K to spend. Knowing what you really have left to spend will help you make better choices.

Subtract Your Expenses

This is where you take away the expenses such as rent, credit card payments, utilities, and so forth from your spendable income. Everything you spend each month, from coffee to your mortgage, goes into the category of expenses. This is going to tell you if you make enough money to cover those expenses.

Organize Your Expenses

Once you have added up all your expenses, one good thing to do is to separate and organize your expenses based on the type of expense. Some expenses are essential and fixed, and some are essential and flexible.

For example, your mortgage is probably a fixed expense that you cannot control once you buy the house. However, the amount you spend on utilities can be a flexible expense even though it is an essential one. Also, some expenses are only periodic. For example, you only pay your property taxes yearly and these are not usually very flexible.

You'll also want to organize all your non-essential expenses, which can be flexible and periodic as well as fixed, just like essential expenses. However, they're not needed for you to stay alive, so they are considered non-essential. They are classified as wants.

One example of a need is a healthy dinner, but the type of dinner you choose to have, if it is more than what is essential for your health, should be classified in your mind as a want.

Track Your Spending

It can help to take some time, such as a month, to track your expenses. However, if you are like most millennials, you use your debit card along with a bank account more than you use cash or checks. This means that you can likely use your online bank account now to look over what you've purchased the last six months to find an average for yourself, without waiting and tracking now.

What you can find out depends on the type of account you have and whether the system is categorizing your expenses correctly. You can go in and fix that, so you can generate reports on your past spending to learn clearly what you are doing with your money.

Track Your Investing

Don't just trust your financial advisor. Look at your accounts, at least monthly, to make sure the money is being deposited and used as you believed it would be when you signed up. By checking and tracking, you can know whether or not you're going to meet the goals you set, and how to adjust (if necessary) to ensure that you do.

Try a Specific Plan

When setting up your budget, it helps to use a specific, tried-and-true budget plan like the 50-20-30 plan created by a Harvard University bankruptcy expert named Elizabeth Warren. This provides a new way to look at your money. This plan makes it super-easy to make spending decisions. Let's look at how this plan works.

Basically, your money is separated into three categories: needs, wants, and savings. 50% should go to your needs, 30 percent to your wants, and 20 percent to savings. The plan is developed on after-tax income. If you work for yourself and pay self-employment taxes, make sure you get your figures right by subtracting your business expenses and state and federal taxes before coming up with your "income" number.

Needs are expenses that are mandatory to live a healthy life – such as a mortgage, utilities, healthcare, basic groceries, transportation, and childcare. Wants include entertainment like cable, phone, eating out, fancy food, personal care like professional hair care, shopping for non-essential items, travel, and so forth. Savings includes everything you save but can consist of student loans and credit card debt, because you should try to pay those off as fast as possible.

This system is flexible because you can use your wants to add to your savings and to upgrade your mandatory expenses. For example, if your budget says you can only live in a $750 apartment but you really want the $1200 apartment, some of that money should come from the "want" category but not your savings category. Also, some of your savings, if you happen to have a lot of debt, can also be included in your want category.

Another plan to check out is a zero-based budget. The way this works is that each month, you zero out your money. So, if you have $5000 each month, you set up a budget that uses every penny so that your income is equal to your expenses every single period, and nothing carries over. This plan is favored by financial experts like Dave Ramsey.

That means that if you end up with a windfall such as a birthday gift or unexpected bonus, you need to create a new budget line for that amount so that you eliminate it from your books. Perhaps you put it in savings or maybe you spend some of it on a new hairstyle, but it should be accounted for in some way.

To make zero-based budgeting work, you'll need to include all your income and your monthly expenses. Everything that spends down the money is considered an expense, including investments and savings. If you start this and you're showing a deficit that is causing you to use credit, it's imperative that you earn more money to cover the extra or cut your expenses.

The main thing is that you create a plan and document it. Write down your plan. Understand your plan and know your plan. Regardless of the method you use, your plan should include both short- and long-term goals so that not only do you take care of today, but you also take care of your future in a realistic way. It's essential that you're honest with yourself about this process.

Use Automation and Technology

One thing that millennials are good at is using technology. You probably already use a lot more automation than your parents and grandparents do. Let's look at the many types of automation and technology that you can use to help manage your money.

- **Your Bank or Credit Union's Tools** – Whatever financial institution you use for your banking needs already has many tools available to you – be it a credit union, bank account, or other account that allows you to add and withdraw money easily without fees. Check them out because you never know what they offer. For example, some offer easy budgeting tools that allow you to set up and track your budget right inside your account. It's good to have it all in one place like that.

- **Financial Management Software** – Cloud-based software in the form of mobile apps like Personal Capital and

Mint.com will enable you to track and manage your finances easily by giving you access to all your accounts in one place. You can also use their financial advisers, get a personalized investment strategy, and more – even tax planning.

- **App to Track Credit Card Awards** – If you have credit cards, many of them come with awards. Most people never use their card benefits because they can't keep track or are unaware of them. Some to check out are Points.com, AwardWallet.com, Stocardapp.com, are Keyringapp.com.

- **Do Use Account Links** – Your financial software often asks you to link up all your accounts. While this takes some time to set up, linking the accounts you use and tracking all the expenses and deposits in one place makes it easier to make decisions at a glance.

- **Automate Tasks** – Depending on your situation, there are many things you can automate. Set up automatic withdrawals for your savings and even bill payments. Automate all your bills to pay the right amount, on time, according to your pay schedule. You'll avoid late fees and even avoid balances if you set up credit cards to pay the entire balance when it's due.

- **Set Up Electronic Reminders** – You may not be able to automate some bills, but you can set up reminders for these so that you don't forget. You can use apps on your smartphone, but you can also sync your phone and computer with Google Calendar with all your reminders. Some of your credit cards' online systems even come with automation features and reminders.

Any automation and technology you choose will work for you if you use it and pay attention to it. It's so much easier, for example, to set up automatic bill payment and investment payments so that you only deal each month with your flexible essential and non-essential expenditures, which means you have less to think about each month.

Simple Savings and Investing Tips

Outside of the money you must spend to live your life, such as shelter, food, healthcare, and so forth, are all non-mandatory expenses that can be classified as wants. If you make savings a mandatory expense, at least in your mind, you can ensure that you're saving enough to meet your goals today and in the future. Let's look at some simple ways to ensure you meet your savings and investing goals.

- **Consumer Debt First** – Other than saving a small amount, such as about $1K for emergencies, start paying off your consumer debt right away. If you have consumer debt, you're canceling out your savings and investments. Don't keep any consumer debt (credit cards, unsecured debt) longer than a few months and only when you've planned it.

- **Round It Up** – There are numerous accounts and cards that will round up every purchase you make and add the cents into a savings account. This is a perfect way to collect money in savings without even thinking about it. There are several apps to try, such as Acorns.com and Wealthfront.com.

- **Budget Your Groceries Better** – It's incredible how healthily you can eat when eating at home. However, many people tend to spend more than they need to on groceries. You can follow a healthy and nutritious plan that saves a lot more than you think. Many people save a few hundred dollars a month once they start budgeting and planning their meals better. Look for low-cost veggie delivery or pick up meal boxes, and more.

- **Watch Your Auto Subscriptions and Memberships** – Today, due to technology, you can be "dollared" to death. A few times a year, double-check all your automatic subscriptions and memberships to make sure you're utilizing them as much as you thought you would.

- **Only Buy Used** – Most things that you need can be found for pennies on the dollar used, and barely used at that. From clothing to furniture, buying used is very good on your wallet. If you're patient, you can find everything you need with few exceptions.

- **Organize What You Have** – When you keep your things organized, you're less likely to buy duplicates. Ensure that you use some of your budget to purchase the right organization tools to keep your stuff well cared for, so it lasts and is in a place that makes it more usable for you.

- **Automate Your Savings** – Once you have decided how much you're saving and investing, don't leave it to chance. Set it up so that it's automatically taken out of your check before you get it, or out of your bank account the moment the money is deposited so that you don't have to think about it.

- **Use Unexpected Income or Windfalls Wisely** – Believe it or not, at some stage almost everyone ends up with some money they did not plan for. When this happens, always use it the smartest way possible, such as by using it for savings or to pay off consumer debt. And if all that is taken care of to your satisfaction, you can use it for something fun.

- **Reduce Your Energy Usage** – One thing you have a lot more control over than you may think is your energy usage. Learn how to save money on electricity by using your dishwasher at less expensive times, wearing your clothing more than once before washing, and using energy-efficient bulbs and appliances.

- **Unsubscribe to Marketing Emails** – It's hard to save when there is temptation everywhere. If you're trying to recover from being an over-spender and you really don't need anything, cancel every marketing email that you get as they come through or use a throwaway free email address when you sign up for things.

- **Borrow More Things** – Don't be a pest, but there is no reason to buy a truck if you only use one twice a year. The same can be said for many things that you only need occasionally. You can borrow from friends and family or even rent a lot of things like that. If you do borrow, take care of it and return it and then do something nice for the buyer.

- **Don't Eat Out** – If you're trying to save for your emergency fund and don't have at least three months of expenses if you're single and six months if you have a partner, then you should not eat out. Eat at home to save money and avoid eating out until you have an emergency fund. Take your lunch to work, and meal plan for home.

- **Pay in Cash** – When you do go shopping, even on vacation or out with friends, take only cash with you. When you only have cash, it's harder to overspend because it's embarrassing not to have enough cash. Using your debit card for every single purchase is fine if you are also keeping track with software, so you know your daily number exactly.

- **Ask about Discounts** – When shopping for anything, don't be afraid to look for and ask directly for discounts. If you don't ask, you won't get it. You can even ask for the "cash price" for medical care and usually save 30 percent or more. Use sites like eBates.com when you must buy new, to help you save money and earn money back.

- **Use Your Work Retirement Savings Plan** – If your work offers a 401K or other type of savings and investing retirement plan, it's imperative that you participate in it. Usually your employer will match a portion of your contribution. It's simple to participate and when the money is just taken from your check before you see it, you don't notice it as much.

- **Lower Your Cell Phone Bill** – You probably don't need as big a plan as you think. Also, there is a lot of competition. At least yearly, call your company to try to get a discount, but don't lock it in. Call around and get more offers.

- **Freeze Non-Essential Spending Temporarily** – One way to ensure that you save for your emergency fund is to stop spending on anything but your essentials such as rent, utilities, food, insurance, and so forth. Don't go to the movies. Don't eat out. Don't buy any extras and stick to the basics for a specified period in order to fund your emergency account.

- **Do More Things Yourself** – If you can do it yourself, do it. Make your own food. Do your own hair. Fix your dishwasher yourself. The more things you can do yourself instead of outsourcing while you're trying to fund your emergency account, the better. You can resume outsourcing once your emergency account is funded and your consumer credit is paid down.

- **Skip the Coffee Shop** – While it's easy to drive through a coffee bar and get that delicious drink, it's too expensive. Just one a day three days a week will add up to about $800 or even a grand a year.

Need motivation? Find an investment calculator and plug that yearly savings number in to find out how much retirement savings you're missing out on. (Hint: If you saved $100 a month for 20 years at a realistic 6 percent interest compounded daily, you'd have almost $50K saved due to the beauty of compound interest.)

- **Use the Library** – Depending on where you live, your library may be a goldmine. Many libraries today have free Wi-Fi, movies, books (including digital and print), and more. They often have programs and even movie nights for activities. Go join your public library and get on the mailing list.

- **Sell Your Junk** – If you have been a consumer up until now, you can also sell the junk you don't use. Even if it's not really "junk", if you don't use it, consider selling it. You can likely put the money you get to good use instead of just housing stuff you never look at or use.

- **Get Creative with Vacations** – Even when you're trying to save money and build your emergency fund, it's important not to stop all the fun forever. Sure, until you have funded the emergency fund and paid off consumer credit, you want to be careful. But you can still have a vacation and have fun. Just get creative about it. Save and plan for it, and don't do it last minute. Consider a staycation but if you do that, become a real tourist in your area and don't just sleep it away.

Like with most things, if you're going to spend your money, always investigate the company or business you are going to work with. Don't just listen to your friends and family; check out the company and the person because scams do happen – even to your friends and family, and you don't want to be a victim.

Money Mistakes to Avoid

Outside of ensuring that you have a budget, using the tools that you can to help you stick to your budget, and saving and investing, there are many mistakes people make with money that you'll want to avoid. Let's look at a few and learn how to avoid them or overcome them.

Living Paycheck to Paycheck

The sad fact is that most people in the USA do live paycheck to paycheck. That means that most people cannot cover the expenses required of them without resorting to credit if they lose their job or an unexpected expense comes up. If you are doing that now, it's imperative that you start managing your money to avoid this.

Using Credit for Everyday Things

Unless you're super-good at paying the entire balance each month and are using the card to gain rewards that add quality to your life, stop using your credit cards for everyday things. If you use a card to buy dinner out (or worse, groceries) because you're short of funds due to another expense, you are in trouble and need to get your budget fixed asap.

Ignoring Student Loans – Instead, Look for Student Loan Programs That Help

So many millennials are having issues with their student loans. Thankfully, there are programs that you can investigate that will help you, at least for the short term. If your income is low enough that you qualify for one of the income-based payment plan options, go ahead and choose that.

These income-based plans allow you to pay a reduced amount if your income qualifies. If you make these payments for 25 years, you don't have to pay off your entire balance at the end of the 25 years but instead will receive a 1099 for the amount owed to claim as income on your taxes.

It's important to understand that in most cases, your payment will not cover the interest, so try to pay that when you get your notifications to avoid your balance increasing while your income is on the low end. Many people on the income-based plan end up eventually earning enough to pay the entire payment instead of qualifying to end payments after 25 years. This means they end up paying back a substantial amount, even up to double their initial balance due to compounding interest.

Even with all the issues, don't ignore notices about your student loans. Typically, you can work out a plan with them based on your situation if only you call and talk to them. Everyone, regardless of income, is currently able to put their loans on temporary forbearance while they gain job experience. There is almost always a way to work it out with them. The one thing you cannot do, at this point in time, is file bankruptcy on your student loans.

Using Credit during Crises

If you're using credit during a crisis and not your emergency savings, you have a serious issue. It's imperative that you do what you can to build your emergency fund. If you still owe on your credit cards, pay minimum payments until you can save at least a grand for emergencies.

Once you have the minimum of a grand in savings, work on paying off one credit card at a time. Once they're done, use the amount you were paying on them to add to your savings until you build three to six months of emergency savings. Then start investing elsewhere.

Remember, your emergency fund is for things that are unexpected, necessary and urgent.

Treating Retirement Savings as an Emergency

Once you have paid off your consumer debt and maximized your emergency savings account with a three to six months emergency fund, it's time to maximize your retirement account contributions. Even though you may think you should not contribute to retirement when you're young, you should.

The sooner you start, the better, due to compounding interest. The truth is, if you started saving just about $450 a month you could have a million dollars in investments (if you earn 6%) in only 20 years. 20 years is going to come fast even if you're in your 20s now. (Try this calculator at Bankrate.com.) Don't think of it as being 20 years from now; think of it as being in the blink of an eye because it's going to happen so much faster than you think.

Putting All Your Eggs in One Basket

It's essential to diversify your investments so that you can mitigate the ups and downs of the market. The easiest way to accomplish this without having to get a master's degree in finance is to find a fund that is named by the date you plan to retire. For example, it may be called the 2045 Fund.

This simply means that the fund is designed and diversified based on the idea that the people in this fund will retire sometime in the 2040s. The investments are made to be concentrated highly in stocks when you're young and to move out of those types of investments closer to retirement. It takes out the guesswork when you allow a fund manager to deal with the ratios.

Ignoring Fees

When you are trying to figure out the best financial fund or investment firm to work with, focus on the fees. Don't let someone tell you that the costs don't matter. They do, and they can be very high and eat away at your investment.

Not Considering What Happens If You're Sick or Gone

It's imperative, especially if you have family counting on you, to ensure that you have adequate life, disability, health, and renters / homeowners insurance. While most people don't want to think about being sick or dying, it does happen. The average life expectancy in the US is almost 79 years, but many things play a role in that average, from access to healthcare to clean air.

Getting Too Serious about What's Hot

During your investing life, you're going to be tempted by a lot of hot deals. However, it's best not to get too carried away by what's hot right now. That doesn't mean you cannot try it out. For example, if you're interested in investing in cryptocurrency, just don't spend more than you're willing to lose. Consider any investments in anything trending and hot to be entertainment.

Not Building Credit History

Many young people don't realize how important it is to build a credit history. Yes, sometimes it seems a little questionable that the way you build credit history is to use credit. But, if you do it responsibly, it'll save you money on your home and anything you need to finance. Focus on your debt to income ratio, opening the right accounts, closing accounts, and how that affects your credit report.

Not Learning about Finance

The truth is, at least in the USA, education about finance is almost non-existent. You'll have to seek out financial literature if you want to learn. But, it's probably one of the most important things you can learn to make your life better.

Not Talking about Money and Your Income with Friends

For some reason, our society has made it seem like bad manners to discuss how much you make with your friends. The problem is that it leads to considerable inequalities in terms of pay. Do talk about your salary and how much things cost with friends and family, so that you know the truth of what's happening out there.

Buying Property without a 20 Percent Down Payment

Yes, you can buy all sorts of property today with nothing down in the USA, but this is what causes problems in the housing market. Before you purchase a home, save the 20 percent down payment. That's going to help keep your head clear about what you can really afford and save you money on private mortgage insurance – which by the way is something you pay for to help out the loan company as it doesn't help you at all.

Buying New Cars

When you want a new automobile, it's tempting to buy a new one. However, it's a waste of money because all cars lose thousands of dollars the moment you drive them off the lot. It takes about four to six years for a vehicle's value drop to stop. If you focus on buying used but well maintained, you'll save lots of money over the years.

Buying Most New Things

In fact, buying most things new is a waste of money. The more items you can find gently used, the more money you're going to save. A well-made sweater that you buy at the thrift store is going to feel just as wonderful, if not more so, than one you paid ten times more for new.

Avoiding Professional Help

The other mistake to avoid making is not seeking out the help of professionals when it comes to your money. Hiring a CFP, CPA, EA, or someone who can genuinely help you with financial planning, including tax planning, will probably literally change your life.

To Sum Up

The good news is that overall, millennials are doing a good job saving money. They're saving more than their parents in their 401Ks at work, and they're trying to be more careful with their money. The lower wages and high cost of necessities like housing, health care, and education are causing some issues, but those can be worked through with a full understanding of how money works.

If you are interested in learning how to use your money effectively, it's within your power to do so by just educating yourself about the realities of personal money management and how savings, credit, and investing really works.

Printed by Libri Plureos GmbH in Hamburg, Germany